Contents

- Introduction
- The Basics
- Vegetarian Mason Jar Salads
- Grain Based Mason Jar Salads
- Protein Packed Mason Jar Salads
- Fruit and Nut Mason Jar Salads
- Seasonal Mason Jar Salads
- Around the World Mason Jar Salads
- Conclusion

Introduction

Welcome, dear reader, to a culinary journey that promises to be as delightful as it is nutritious. This isn't just a cookbook; it's an invitation to explore the vibrant world of mason jar salads, where health and convenience meet in a symphony of colors and flavors.

Picture this: a busy weekday morning. You're rushing to get out the door, and there's no time to prepare a healthy lunch. But wait, there in your fridge is a mason jar salad, prepared in advance, brimming with fresh, nutritious ingredients. You grab it, and you're on your way. No stress, no mess, just a delicious meal waiting for you when hunger strikes.

That's the magic of mason jar salads. They're not just meals; they're lifelines for those of us striving to maintain a healthy diet amidst the hustle and bustle of modern life. They're proof that fast food can be good food, and that eating well doesn't have to be a chore.

In this book, we'll explore the endless possibilities that mason jar salads offer. From protein-packed powerhouses to light and refreshing veggie delights, there's a mason jar salad for every taste, every mood, and every dietary need.

But this book is about more than just recipes. It's about empowering you to take control of your health, one mason jar at a time. It's about showing you that with a little bit of planning and a lot of creativity, you can turn simple ingredients into meals that nourish your body and delight your palate.

We'll start with the basics, introducing you to the staple ingredients that make mason jar salads so versatile and satisfying. We'll explore the world of homemade dressings, where a handful of ingredients can transform a simple salad into a flavor-packed feast.

Then, we'll dive into the recipes. Each one has been carefully crafted to provide a balance of nutrients, ensuring that every bite is as good for you as it is delicious. And with a variety of vegetarian, protein-packed, grain-based, fruit and nut, and seasonal options, there's something for everyone.

For our vegetarian friends, we've curated a selection of plant-based salads that are as hearty as they are flavorful. From crisp greens to creamy beans, these salads prove that you don't need meat to make a meal satisfying.

If you're looking to up your protein intake, our protein-packed salads are just the ticket. Featuring ingredients like lean chicken, tofu, and a variety of beans, these salads will keep you fueled and satisfied all day long.

Our grain-based salads are a testament to the power of whole grains. Quinoa, farro, brown rice - these are just a few of the hearty grains that can turn a simple salad into a filling meal.

For those with a sweet tooth, our fruit and nut salads offer a delightful blend of sweet and savory flavors. Crunchy nuts, sweet fruits, and a variety of greens come together in these salads to create a meal that's as satisfying as it is delicious.

And finally, our seasonal salads celebrate the bounty of each season. From the fresh greens of spring to the hearty root vegetables of winter, these salads are a delicious way to eat with the seasons.

But this book isn't just about following recipes. It's about inspiring you to create your own. With each recipe, we'll provide tips and suggestions for substitutions and additions, empowering you to customize each salad to your liking.

We'll also provide guidance on how to layer your mason jar salads to ensure maximum freshness.

You see, the secret to a perfect mason jar salad lies in the layering. Dressing at the bottom, followed by hardier ingredients that can withstand a bit of marinating, and then the lighter ingredients, with your leafy greens at the top. This way, everything stays crisp and fresh, and your salad is perfectly mixed when you're ready to eat.

We'll also delve into the art of meal prepping. With a bit of planning and a couple of hours on a Sunday afternoon, you can prepare a week's worth of salads, ensuring you always have a healthy meal at hand.

And let's not forget about the mason jars themselves. These humble glass containers are not only practical, but they're also sustainable. They're reusable, durable, and dishwasher safe. Plus, their clear glass walls provide a beautiful display for your colorful salads.

But enough about what's to come. Let's talk about why we're here. Why mason jar salads? Why not just a regular salad in a regular bowl? Well, dear reader, the answer is simple: convenience and longevity.

Mason jar salads are the ultimate grab-and-go meal. They're compact, easy to transport, and can be eaten straight from the jar. No need for separate containers for your salad and dressing. Everything is right there, ready to be mixed and enjoyed.

And when it comes to longevity, mason jar salads reign supreme. Thanks to the layering method we'll teach you, your salads can stay fresh for up to a week. That's right, a week! Say goodbye to wilted greens and soggy vegetables. With mason jar salads, every bite is as fresh as the first.

So, whether you're a seasoned salad lover or a newbie looking to incorporate more greens into your diet, this book is for you. It's for the busy parent looking for quick and healthy meal options. It's for the office worker tired of fast food lunches. It's for the fitness enthusiast looking for protein-packed post-workout meals.

It's for the environmentally conscious consumer looking for sustainable meal options. It's for the adventurous eater looking to expand their culinary horizons. But most of all, it's for you, dear reader, because everyone deserves to enjoy delicious, nutritious meals, no matter how busy life gets.

As you flip through these pages, we hope you feel inspired to try new ingredients, experiment with flavors, and most importantly, have fun. Cooking isn't just about nourishing our bodies; it's about nourishing our souls. It's about taking a moment to slow down, to savor, to enjoy.

So, grab your mason jars, roll up your sleeves, and let's get started. A world of flavor awaits you, and we can't wait to see what delicious creations you'll come up with.

Remember, there's no right or wrong way to make a salad. It's all about what makes you feel good, both inside and out. So, don't be afraid to experiment, to customize, to make these recipes your own.

Most importantly, remember to enjoy the process. The chopping of the vegetables, the whisking of the dressing, the layering of the ingredients - these are all acts of self-care, small moments of mindfulness in our busy lives.

So, here's to health, to convenience, to delicious meals enjoyed anywhere and everywhere. Here's to mason jar salads, the humble heroes of the culinary world.

We hope this book inspires you, empowers you, and most importantly, helps you discover the joy of healthy eating. Because at the end of the day, that's what it's all about: finding joy in the food we eat and the way we live. It's about making choices that make us feel good, that nourish our bodies and our souls. It's about embracing the beautiful messiness of life and finding ways to make it a little bit easier, a little bit tastier.

The Basics

1As we embark on this culinary adventure, it's important to start with a solid foundation. In the world of mason jar salads, that foundation is built on a selection of staple ingredients. These are the building blocks from which we'll create a myriad of delicious, nutritious meals.

Let's start with **the greens**. The beauty of salads is their versatility, and that starts with the variety of leafy greens available to us. From the crisp, mild flavor of romaine lettuce to the peppery bite of arugula, the choice of greens can dramatically change the flavor profile of your salad.

Spinach, with its delicate leaves and slightly sweet flavor, is a great source of iron and pairs well with virtually any dressing. **Kale**, on the other hand, is hardier with a slightly bitter flavor, packed with nutrients, and stands up well to robust dressings.

Then there are **the grains. Quinoa**, with its slightly nutty flavor and high protein content, is a popular choice. **Brown rice, farro, and barley** are also excellent options, adding a hearty element to your salads that will keep you feeling full longer.

Next, let's talk about **proteins**. For meat-eaters, grilled **chicken, turkey, or shrimp** can add a savory element to your salads. For vegetarians and vegans, **beans, tofu, and tempeh** are excellent sources of protein.

Beans, in particular, are a salad superstar. **Black beans, chickpeas, kidney beans, and lentils** not only add a protein punch but also provide a satisfying texture contrast. Plus, they're incredibly versatile, taking on the flavors of the ingredients around them.

Now, onto the **veggies**. The options here are virtually limitless. Crunchy **bell peppers, juicy tomatoes, crisp cucumbers, sweet corn** - the choice is yours. Just remember, the more colorful your salad, the wider the range of nutrients you're getting.

And let's not forget about **fruits**. Sliced **strawberries, crisp apples, juicy oranges, and sweet grapes** can add a refreshing sweetness to your salads. Plus, they're packed with vitamins and antioxidants.

Nuts and seeds add a delightful crunch to your salads, not to mention a healthy dose of good fats. **Almonds, walnuts, sunflower seeds, chia seeds** - these little powerhouses can transform a simple salad into a nutrient-dense meal.

Finally, we have the **dressings**. These are the magic potions that bring your salads to life. A good dressing can elevate your salad from good to great, and the best part is, they're incredibly easy to make at home.

Let's start with a classic: the **vinaigrette**. At its most basic, a vinaigrette is a mixture of **oil and vinegar**. But with a little creativity, you can create a wide variety of vinaigrettes to suit any salad.

For a basic vinaigrette, you'll need 3 parts oil to 1 part vinegar. **Olive oil and white wine vinegar** are a classic combination, but don't be afraid to experiment. Try using different types of vinegar, like **balsamic or apple cider**, or different types of oil, like **avocado or walnut**.

To your oil and vinegar, you can add a variety of flavorings. **Dijon mustard** adds a tangy kick and helps emulsify the dressing. **Honey or maple syrup** adds a touch of sweetness. **Fresh or dried herbs, garlic, shallots, citrus zest** - the possibilities are endless.

Next, let's talk about **creamy dressings.** These are the dressings that coat your salad ingredients in a layer of creamy goodness. Think ranch, Caesar, or blue cheese. But don't worry, you don't need to rely on store-bought versions. You can make healthier versions at home with a few simple ingredients.

Assembling your mason jar salads:

The dressing goes in first. This ensures that your salad ingredients don't get soggy, and it makes it easy to mix your salad when you're ready to eat. Just pour the dressing into the bottom of the jar, then layer your ingredients on top.

Speaking of layering, let's talk about the best way to layer your salad ingredients. After the dressing, add your hardier ingredients. These are ingredients that can withstand sitting in dressing for a few days without getting soggy. Think beans, cucumbers, bell peppers, or grains.

Next, add your protein, followed by any softer veggies or fruits. These are ingredients that can get a bit soggy if they sit in dressing for too long, so it's best to keep them away from the dressing until you're ready to eat.

Finally, add your greens. These should always go on top to keep them away from the dressing and ensure they stay crisp and fresh.

When you're ready to eat, just give your jar a good shake to distribute the dressing, then pour it into a bowl or eat it straight from the jar. The choice is yours!

Want to try a Mexican-inspired salad? Try layering black beans, corn, avocado, tomato, and cilantro over a bed of romaine lettuce, then top it with a lime vinaigrette. Craving something sweet and savory? Try a salad of spinach, strawberries, goat cheese, and almonds, topped with a balsamic vinaigrette.

The possibilities are endless, and that's part of the fun. So don't be afraid to get creative, to try new combinations, to make these salads your own.

Remember, the goal is to create meals that you enjoy, that satisfy your hunger, and that make you feel good. So listen to your body, pay attention to what it's craving

And most importantly, have fun with it. Cooking is an art, a form of self-expression. It's a chance to get creative, to play with flavors and textures, to create something beautiful and delicious. So embrace the process, enjoy the journey, and savor every bite.

As we move forward in this book, we'll provide you with a variety of recipes to get you started. But these are just a starting point. We encourage you to use them as inspiration, as a jumping-off point for your own culinary creations.

Vegetarian Mason Jar Salads

Welcome to the world of Vegetarian Mason Jar Salads, a vibrant realm where plants take center stage. This section is dedicated to those who believe in the power of plant-based eating, and to those who simply want to incorporate more veggies into their diet. Whether you're a lifelong vegetarian, a dedicated vegan, or just a curious omnivore, these salads are for you.

QUINOA AND BLACK BEAN SALAD

DRESSING INGREDIENTS

- 2 tbsp olive oil
- 1 tbsp lime juice
- 1 tsp cumin
- Salt and pepper to taste

SALAD INGREDIENTS

- 1 cup cooked quinoa
- 1 cup black beans
- 1 cup corn
- 1 diced bell pepper
- 1/2 cup diced red onion

METHOD

- Mix dressing ingredients in a small bowl.
- Layer ingredients in mason jar starting with dressing, then quinoa, beans, corn, bell pepper, and onion.
- Seal and refrigerate until ready to eat.
- Shake before serving.

GREEK SALAD

DRESSING INGREDIENTS

- 3 tbsp olive oil
- 1 tbsp red wine vinegar
- 1 tsp dried oregano
- Salt and pepper to taste

SALAD INGREDIENTS

- 1 cup diced cucumber
- 1 cup cherry tomatoes
- 1/2 cup sliced olives
- 1/2 cup feta cheese
- 1/2 cup diced red onion

METHOD

- Mix dressing ingredients in a small bowl.
- Layer ingredients in mason jar starting with dressing, then cucumber, tomatoes, olives, feta, and onion.
- Seal and refrigerate until ready to eat.
- Shake before serving.

ASIAN NOODLE SALAD

DRESSING INGREDIENTS

- 2 tbsp sesame oil
- 1 tbsp soy sauce
- 1 tbsp rice vinegar
- 1 tsp honey
- 1 tsp grated ginger

SALAD INGREDIENTS

- 1 cup cooked soba noodles
- 1 cup shredded carrots
- 1 cup sliced bell peppers
- 1/2 cup edamame
- 1/2 cup sliced green onions

METHOD

- Mix dressing ingredients in a small bowl.
- Layer ingredients in mason jar starting with dressing, then noodles, carrots, bell peppers, edamame, and green onions.
- Seal and refrigerate until ready to eat.
- Shake before serving.

CAPRESE SALAD

DRESSING INGREDIENTS

- 3 tbsp olive oil
- 1 tbsp balsamic vinegar
- Salt and pepper to taste

SALAD INGREDIENTS

- 1 cup cherry tomatoes
- 1 cup mozzarella balls
- 1/2 cup fresh basil leaves

METHOD

- Mix dressing ingredients in a small bowl.
- Layer ingredients in mason jar starting with dressing, then cherry tomatoes, mozzarella and basil.
- Seal and refrigerate until ready to eat.
- Shake before serving.

SOUTHWEST SALAD

DRESSING INGREDIENTS

- 2 tbsp olive oil
- 1 tbsp lime juice
- 1 tsp chili powder
- Salt and pepper to taste

SALAD INGREDIENTS

- 1 cup cooked quinoa
- 1 cup black beans
- 1 cup corn
- 1 diced bell pepper
- 1/2 cup diced red onion

METHOD

- Mix dressing ingredients in a small bowl.
- Layer ingredients in mason jar starting with dressing, then quinoa, black beans, corn, bell pepper and red onion.
- Seal and refrigerate until ready to eat.
- Shake before serving.

RAINBOW SALAD

DRESSING INGREDIENTS

- 3 tbsp olive oil
- 1 tbsp apple cider vinegar
- 1 tsp honey
- Salt and pepper to taste

SALAD INGREDIENTS

- 1 cup shredded red cabbage
- 1 cup shredded carrots
- 1 cup diced cucumber
- 1/2 cup cherry tomatoes
- 1/2 cup diced red onion

METHOD

- Mix dressing ingredients in a small bowl.
- Layer ingredients in mason jar starting with dressing, then red cabbage, carrots, cucumber, tomatoes and red onion.
- Seal and refrigerate until ready to eat.
- Shake before serving.

MEDITERRANEAN CHICKPEA SALAD

DRESSING INGREDIENTS

- 3 tbsp olive oil
- 1 tbsp lemon juice
- 1 tsp dried oregano
- Salt and pepper to taste

SALAD INGREDIENTS

- 1 cup chickpeas
- 1 cup diced cucumber
- 1/2 cup diced red onion
- 1/2 cup feta cheese
- 1/2 cup sliced olives

METHOD

- Mix dressing ingredients in a small bowl.
- Layer ingredients in mason jar starting with dressing, then chickpeas, cucumber, red onion, feta and olives.
- Seal and refrigerate until ready to eat.
- Shake before serving.

SPINACH AND STRAWBERRY SALAD

DRESSING INGREDIENTS

- 2 tbsp olive oil
- 1 tbsp balsamic vinegar
- 1 tsp honey
- Salt and pepper to taste

SALAD INGREDIENTS

- 2 cups spinach
- 1 cup sliced strawberries
- 1/2 cup goat cheese
- 1/4 cup sliced almonds

METHOD

- Mix dressing ingredients in a small bowl.
- Layer ingredients in mason jar starting with dressing, then spinach, strawberries, goat cheese and almonds.
- Seal and refrigerate until ready to eat.
- Shake before serving.

BROCCOLI AND CRANBERRY SALAD

DRESSING INGREDIENTS

- 2 tbsp olive oil
- 1 tbsp apple cider vinegar
- 1 tsp honey
- Salt and pepper to taste

SALAD INGREDIENTS

- 2 cups broccoli florets
- 1/2 cup dried cranberries
- 1/2 cup sunflower seeds
- 1/2 cup diced red onion

METHOD

- Mix dressing ingredients in a small bowl.
- Layer ingredients in mason jar starting with dressing, then broccoli, cranberries, sunflower seeds and red onion.
- Seal and refrigerate until ready to eat.
- Shake before serving.

BEET AND GOAT CHEESE SALAD

DRESSING INGREDIENTS

- 2 tbsp olive oil
- 1 tbsp balsamic vinegar
- 1 tsp honey
- Salt and pepper to taste

SALAD INGREDIENTS

- 2 cups mixed greens
- 1 cup roasted beets
- 1/2 cup goat cheese
- 1/4 cup walnuts

METHOD

- Mix dressing ingredients in a small bowl.
- Layer ingredients in mason jar starting with dressing, then mixed greens, beets, goat cheese and walnuts.
- Seal and refrigerate until ready to eat.
- Shake before serving.

Grain Based Mason Jar Salads

Welcome to the hearty world of grain-based mason jar salads. This section is dedicated to salads that feature the wholesome goodness of grains as their star ingredient. From the nutty nuances of quinoa to the comforting familiarity of brown rice, grains bring a satisfying depth to our salads that is both nourishing and fulfilling.

QUINOA AND AVOCADO SALAD

DRESSING INGREDIENTS

- 2 tbsp olive oil
- 1 tbsp lemon juice
- Salt and pepper to taste

SALAD INGREDIENTS

- 1 cup cooked quinoa
- 1 diced avocado
- 1 cup cherry tomatoes
- 1/2 cup diced cucumber
- 1/2 cup diced red onion

METHOD

- -Mix dressing ingredients in a small bowl.
- Layer ingredients in mason jar starting with dressing, then quinoa, avocado, tomatoes, cucumber, and onion.
- Seal and refrigerate until ready to eat.
- Shake before serving.

FARRO AND ROASTED VEGGIE SALAD

DRESSING INGREDIENTS

- 3 tbsp olive oil
- 1 tbsp balsamic vinegar
- Salt and pepper to taste

SALAD INGREDIENTS

- – 1 cup cooked farro
- 1 cup roasted vegetables of your choice
- 1/2 cup feta cheese
- 1/2 cup diced red onion

METHOD

- Mix dressing ingredients in a small bowl.
- Layer ingredients in mason jar starting with dressing, then farro, vegetables, feta, and onion
- Seal and refrigerate until ready to eat.
- Shake before serving.

BARLEY AND MUSHROOM SALAD

DRESSING INGREDIENTS

- 2 tbsp olive oil
- 1 tbsp apple cider vinegar
- 1 tsp Dijon mustard
- Salt and pepper to taste

SALAD INGREDIENTS

- 1 cup cooked barley
- 1 cup sautéed mushrooms
- 1/2 cup diced red onion
- 1/2 cup diced bell pepper

METHOD

- Mix dressing ingredients in a small bowl.
- Layer ingredients in mason jar starting with dressing, then barley, mushrooms, onion, and bell pepper.
- Seal and refrigerate until ready to eat.
- Shake before serving.

COUSCOUS AND CHICKPEA SALAD

DRESSING INGREDIENTS

- 3 tbsp olive oil
- 1 tbsp lemon juice
- 1 tsp dried oregano
- Salt and pepper to taste

SALAD INGREDIENTS

- 1 cup cooked couscous
- 1 cup chickpeas
- 1 cup diced cucumber
- 1/2 cup diced red onion
- 1/2 cup feta cheese

METHOD

- Mix dressing ingredients in a small bowl.
- Layer ingredients in mason jar starting with dressing, then couscous, chickpeas, cucumber, onion, and feta.
- Seal and refrigerate until ready to eat.
- Shake before serving.

BROWN RICE AND EDAMAME SALAD

DRESSING INGREDIENTS

- 2 tbsp sesame oil
- 1 tbsp soy sauce
- 1 tbsp rice vinegar
- 1 tsp honey

SALAD INGREDIENTS

- 1 cup cooked brown rice
- 1 cup shelled edamame
- 1 cup shredded carrots
- 1/2 cup diced red bell pepper
- 1/2 cup sliced green onions

METHOD

- Mix dressing ingredients in a small bowl.
- Layer ingredients in mason jar starting with dressing, then rice, edamame, carrots, bell pepper, and green onions
- Seal and refrigerate until ready to eat.
- Shake before serving.

BULGUR AND LENTIL SALAD

DRESSING INGREDIENTS

- 3 tbsp olive oil
- 1 tbsp lemon juice
- 1 tsp cumin
- Salt and pepper to taste

SALAD INGREDIENTS

- 1 cup cooked bulgur
- 1 cup cooked lentils
- 1 cup diced cucumber
- 1/2 cup diced red onion
- 1/2 cup diced bell pepper

METHOD

- Mix dressing ingredients in a small bowl.
- Layer ingredients in mason jar starting with dressing, then bulgur, lentils, cucumber, onion, and bell pepper.
-
- Seal and refrigerate until ready to eat.
- Shake before serving.

MILLET AND ROASTED BEET SALAD

DRESSING INGREDIENTS

- 2 tbsp olive oil
- 1 tbsp apple cider vinegar
- 1 tsp honey
- Salt and pepper to taste

SALAD INGREDIENTS

- 1 cup cooked millet
- 1 cup roasted beets
- 1/2 cup goat cheese
- 1/2 cup arugula

METHOD

- Mix dressing ingredients in a small bowl.
- Layer ingredients in mason jar starting with dressing, then millet, beets, cheese, and arugula.
- Seal and refrigerate until ready to eat.
- Shake before serving.

WILD RICE AND CRANBERRY SALAD

DRESSING INGREDIENTS

- 3 tbsp olive oil
- 1 tbsp balsamic vinegar
- 1 tsp honey
- Salt and pepper to taste

SALAD INGREDIENTS

- 1 cup cooked wild rice
- 1 cup dried cranberries
- 1/2 cup diced celery
- 1/2 cup diced red onion
- 1/2 cup chopped pecans

METHOD

- Mix dressing ingredients in a small bowl
- Layer ingredients in mason jar starting with dressing, then rice, cranberries, celery, onion, and pecans.
- Seal and refrigerate until ready to eat.
- Shake before serving.

SPELT AND ROASTED SQUASH SALAD

DRESSING INGREDIENTS

- 2 tbsp olive oil
-
- 1 tbsp apple cider vinegar
- 1 tsp Dijon mustard
- Salt and pepper to taste

SALAD INGREDIENTS

- - 1 cup cooked spelt
- 1 cup roasted squash
- 1/2 cup crumbled blue cheese
- 1/2 cup chopped walnuts

METHOD

- Mix dressing ingredients in a small bowl
- Layer ingredients in mason jar starting with dressing, then spelt, squash, cheese, and walnuts
- Seal and refrigerate until ready to eat.
- Shake before serving.

AMARANTH AND BLACK BEAN SALAD

DRESSING INGREDIENTS

- 2 tbsp olive oil
- 1 tbsp lime juice
- 1 tsp cumin
- Salt and pepper to taste

SALAD INGREDIENTS

- 1 cup cooked amaranth
- 1 cup black beans
- 1 cup corn
- 1/2 cup diced bell pepper
- 1/2 cup diced red onion

METHOD

- Mix dressing ingredients in a small bowl.
- Layer ingredients in mason jar starting with dressing, then amaranth, beans, corn, bell pepper, and onion.
- Seal and refrigerate until ready to eat.
- Shake before serving.

Protein Packed Mason Jar Salads

Welcome to the section where power meets flavor: Protein-Packed Mason Jar Salads. In this part of our culinary journey, we'll explore how to create salads that are not only delicious and nutritious but also loaded with protein to keep you fueled throughout your day. Whether you're a fitness enthusiast looking for a post-workout meal, a busy professional needing sustained energy, or simply someone who enjoys a hearty salad, this section is for you.

CHICKEN CAESAR SALAD

DRESSING INGREDIENTS

- 2 tbsp olive oil
- 1 tbsp lemon juice
- 1 tsp Dijon mustard
- Salt and pepper to taste

SALAD INGREDIENTS

- 2 cups romaine lettuce
- 1 cup grilled chicken diced
- 1/2 cup croutons
- 1/4 cup parmesan cheese

METHOD

- Mix dressing ingredients in a small bowl.
- Layer ingredients in mason jar starting with dressing, then chicken, croutons, cheese, and lettuce.
- Seal and refrigerate until ready to eat.
- Shake before serving.

TUNA SALAD

DRESSING INGREDIENTS

- 3 tbsp olive oil
- 1 tbsp red wine vinegar
- Salt and pepper to taste

SALAD INGREDIENTS

- 2 cups mixed greens
- 1 can tuna drained
- 1/2 cup diced cucumber
- 1/2 cup cherry tomatoes

METHOD

- Mix dressing ingredients in a small bowl.
- Layer ingredients in mason jar starting with dressing, then tuna, cucumber, tomatoes, and greens.
- Seal and refrigerate until ready to eat.
- Shake before serving.

QUINOA AND CHICKPEA SALAD

DRESSING INGREDIENTS

- 2 tbsp olive oil
- 1 tbsp lemon juice
- 1 tsp cumin
- Salt and pepper to taste

SALAD INGREDIENTS

- 1 cup cooked quinoa
- 1 cup chickpeas
- 1 cup diced bell pepper
- 1/2 cup diced red onion

METHOD

- Mix dressing ingredients in a small bowl.
- Layer ingredients in mason jar starting with dressing, then quinoa, chickpeas, bell pepper, and onion.
- Seal and refrigerate until ready to eat.
- Shake before serving.

STEAK AND BLUE CHEESE SALAD

DRESSING INGREDIENTS

- 3 tbsp olive oil
- 1 tbsp balsamic vinegar
- Salt and pepper to taste

SALAD INGREDIENTS

- 2 cups spinach
- 1 cup grilled steak sliced
- 1/2 cup blue cheese
- 1/4 cup walnuts

METHOD

- Mix dressing ingredients in a small bowl.
- Layer ingredients in mason jar starting with dressing, then steak, cheese, walnuts, and spinach.
- Seal and refrigerate until ready to eat.
- Shake before serving.

GREEK CHICKEN SALAD

DRESSING INGREDIENTS

- 3 tbsp olive oil
- 1 tbsp red wine vinegar
- 1 tsp dried oregano
- Salt and pepper to taste

SALAD INGREDIENTS

- 2 cups romaine lettuce
- 1 cup grilled chicken diced
- 1/2 cup feta cheese
- 1/2 cup diced cucumber
- 1/2 cup cherry tomatoes

METHOD

- Mix dressing ingredients in a small bowl.
- Layer ingredients in mason jar starting with dressing, then chicken, feta, cucumber, tomatoes, and lettuce.
- Seal and refrigerate until ready to eat.
- Shake before serving.

SHRIMP AND AVOCADO SALAD

DRESSING INGREDIENTS

- 2 tbsp olive oil
- 1 tbsp lime juice
- Salt and pepper to taste

SALAD INGREDIENTS

- 2 cups mixed greens
- 1 cup cooked shrimp
- 1/2 cup diced avocado
- 1/2 cup cherry tomatoes

METHOD

- Mix dressing ingredients in a small bowl.
- Layer ingredients in mason jar starting with dressing, then shrimp, avocado, tomatoes, and greens.
- Seal and refrigerate until ready to eat.
- Shake before serving.

TURKEY AND CRANBERRY SALAD

DRESSING INGREDIENTS

- 3 tbsp olive oil
- 1 tbsp apple cider vinegar
- 1 tsp honey
- Salt and pepper to taste

SALAD INGREDIENTS

- 2 cups spinach
- 1 cup turkey breast diced
- 1/2 cup dried cranberries
- 1/4 cup walnuts

METHOD

- Mix dressing ingredients in a small bowl.
- Layer ingredients in mason jar starting with dressing, then turkey, cranberries, walnuts, and spinach.
- Seal and refrigerate until ready to eat.
- Shake before serving.

SALMON AND ASPARAGUS SALAD

DRESSING INGREDIENTS

- 2 tbsp olive oil
- 1 tbsp lemon juice
- Salt and pepper to taste

SALAD INGREDIENTS

- 2 cups mixed greens
- 1 cup grilled salmon flaked
- 1/2 cup grilled asparagus chopped
- 1/4 cup sliced almonds

METHOD

- Mix dressing ingredients in a small bowl.
- Layer ingredients in mason jar starting with dressing, then salmon, asparagus, almonds, and greens.
- Seal and refrigerate until ready to eat.
- Shake before serving.

HAM AND CHEESE SALAD

DRESSING INGREDIENTS

- 3 tbsp olive oil
- 1 tbsp apple cider vinegar
- Salt and pepper to taste

SALAD INGREDIENTS

- 2 cups romaine lettuce
- 1 cup ham diced
- 1/2 cup cheddar cheese diced
- 1/2 cup cherry tomatoes

METHOD

- Mix dressing ingredients in a small bowl.
- Layer ingredients in mason jar starting with dressing, then ham, cheese, tomatoes, and lettuce.
- Seal and refrigerate until ready to eat.
- Shake before serving.

EGG AND BACON SALAD

DRESSING INGREDIENTS

- 2 tbsp olive oil
- 1 tbsp apple cider vinegar
- Salt and pepper to taste

SALAD INGREDIENTS

- 2 cups spinach
- 2 hard-boiled eggs sliced,
- 1/2 cup cooked bacon crumbled
- 1/4 cup cherry tomatoes

METHOD

- Mix dressing ingredients in a small bowl.
- Layer ingredients in mason jar starting with dressing, then eggs, bacon, tomatoes, and spinach.
- Seal and refrigerate until ready to eat.
- Shake before serving.

Fruit and Nut Mason Jar Salads

Welcome to the world of Fruit and Nut Mason Jar Salads, where the line between meal and dessert blurs in the most delightful way. This section is a celebration of nature's candy - fruits, and their perfect partners, nuts. Here, we'll explore the sweet, the savory, and the crunchy, creating salads that are as pleasing to the palate as they are to the eye.

APPLE WALNUT SALAD

DRESSING INGREDIENTS

- 2 tbsp olive oil
- 1 tbsp apple cider vinegar
- 1 tsp honey
- Salt and pepper to taste

SALAD INGREDIENTS

- 2 cups mixed greens
- 1 diced apple
- 1/2 cup walnuts
- 1/2 cup blue cheese

METHOD

- Mix dressing ingredients in a small bowl.
- Layer ingredients in mason jar starting with dressing, then greens, apple, walnuts, and cheese.
- Seal and refrigerate until ready to eat.
- Shake before serving.

STRAWBERRY ALMOND SALAD

DRESSING INGREDIENTS

- 2 tbsp olive oil
- 1 tbsp balsamic vinegar
- 1 tsp honey
- Salt and pepper to taste

SALAD INGREDIENTS

- 2 cups spinach
- 1 cup sliced strawberries
- 1/2 cup almonds
- 1/2 cup goat cheese

METHOD

- Mix dressing ingredients in a small bowl.
- Layer ingredients in mason jar starting with dressing, then spinach, strawberries, almonds, and cheese.
- Seal and refrigerate until ready to eat.
- Shake before serving.

TROPICAL FRUIT SALAD

DRESSING INGREDIENTS

- 2 tbsp coconut oil
- 1 tbsp lime juice
- 1 tsp honey
- Salt to taste

SALAD INGREDIENTS

- 1 cup diced mango
- 1 cup diced pineapple
- 1/2 cup shredded coconut
- 1/2 cup macadamia nuts

METHOD

- Mix dressing ingredients in a small bowl.
- Layer ingredients in mason jar starting with dressing, then mango, pineapple, coconut, and nuts.
- Seal and refrigerate until ready to eat.
- Shake before serving.

BERRY PECAN SALAD

DRESSING INGREDIENTS

- 2 tbsp olive oil
- 1 tbsp raspberry vinegar
- 1 tsp honey
- Salt and pepper to taste

SALAD INGREDIENTS

- 2 cups mixed greens
- 1 cup mixed berries
- 1/2 cup pecans
- 1/2 cup feta cheese

METHOD

- Mix dressing ingredients in a small bowl.
- Layer ingredients in mason jar starting with dressing, then greens, berries, pecans, and cheese.
- Seal and refrigerate until ready to eat.
- Shake before serving.

PEAR AND GORGONZOLA SALAD

DRESSING INGREDIENTS

- 2 tbsp olive oil
- 1 tbsp balsamic vinegar
- 1 tsp honey
- Salt and pepper to taste

SALAD INGREDIENTS

- 2 cups mixed greens
- 1 diced pear
- 1/2 cup walnuts
- 1/2 cup gorgonzola cheese

METHOD

- Mix dressing ingredients in a small bowl.
- Layer ingredients in mason jar starting with dressing, then greens, pear, walnuts, and cheese.
- Seal and refrigerate until ready to eat.
- Shake before serving.

PEACH AND ALMOND SALAD

DRESSING INGREDIENTS

- 2 tbsp olive oil
- 1 tbsp apple cider vinegar
- 1 tsp honey
- Salt and pepper to taste

SALAD INGREDIENTS

- 2 cups spinach
- 1 diced peach
- 1/2 cup almonds
- 1/2 cup goat cheese

METHOD

- Mix dressing ingredients in a small bowl.
- Layer ingredients in mason jar starting with dressing, then spinach, peach, almonds, and cheese.
- Seal and refrigerate until ready to eat.
- Shake before serving.

CHERRY AND PISTACHIO SALAD

DRESSING INGREDIENTS

- 2 tbsp olive oil
- 1 tbsp balsamic vinegar
- 1 tsp honey
- Salt and pepper to taste

SALAD INGREDIENTS

- 2 cups mixed greens
- 1 cup pitted cherries
- 1/2 cup pistachios
- 1/2 cup feta cheese

METHOD

- Mix dressing ingredients in a small bowl.
- Layer ingredients in mason jar starting with dressing, then greens, cherries, pistachios, and cheese.
- Seal and refrigerate until ready to eat.
- Shake before serving.

BLUEBERRY AND WALNUT SALAD

DRESSING INGREDIENTS

- 2 tbsp olive oil
- 1 tbsp lemon juice
- 1 tsp honey
- Salt and pepper to taste

SALAD INGREDIENTS

- 2 cups spinach
- 1 cup blueberries
- 1/2 cup walnuts
- 1/2 cup goat cheese

METHOD

- Mix dressing ingredients in a small bowl.
- Layer ingredients in mason jar starting with dressing, then spinach, blueberries, walnuts, and cheese.
- Seal and refrigerate until ready to eat.
- Shake before serving.

RASPBERRY AND ALMOND SALAD

DRESSING INGREDIENTS

- 2 tbsp olive oil
- 1 tbsp raspberry vinegar
- 1 tsp honey
- Salt and pepper to taste

SALAD INGREDIENTS

- 2 cups mixed greens
- 1 cup raspberries
- 1/2 cup almonds
- 1/2 cup feta cheese

METHOD

- Mix dressing ingredients in a small bowl.
- Layer ingredients in mason jar starting with dressing, then greens, raspberries, almonds, and cheese.
- Seal and refrigerate until ready to eat.
- Shake before serving.

GRAPE AND PECAN SALAD

DRESSING INGREDIENTS

- 2 tbsp olive oil
- 1 tbsp balsamic vinegar
- 1 tsp honey
- Salt and pepper to taste

SALAD INGREDIENTS

- 2 cups mixed greens
- 1 cup halved grapes
- 1/2 cup pecans
- 1/2 cup blue cheese

METHOD

- Mix dressing ingredients in a small bowl.
- Layer ingredients in mason jar starting with dressing, then greens, grapes, pecans, and cheese.
- Seal and refrigerate until ready to eat.
- Shake before serving.

Seasonal Mason Jar Salads

As we journey through the year, each season brings with it a unique bounty of fresh produce. From the vibrant greens of spring to the hearty root vegetables of winter, eating seasonally allows us to enjoy a variety of flavors while also maximizing the nutritional value of our meals.

SPRING GREENS SALAD

DRESSING INGREDIENTS

- 3 tbsp olive oil
- 1 tbsp lemon juice
- Salt and pepper to taste

SALAD INGREDIENTS

- 2 cups mixed spring greens
- 1 cup sliced radishes
- 1 cup peas
- 1/2 cup feta cheese

METHOD

- Mix dressing ingredients in a small bowl.
- Layer ingredients in mason jar starting with dressing, then greens, radishes, peas, and feta.
- Seal and refrigerate until ready to eat.
- Shake before serving.

SUMMER BERRY SALAD

DRESSING INGREDIENTS

- 2 tbsp olive oil
- 1 tbsp balsamic vinegar
- 1 tsp honey

SALAD INGREDIENTS

- 2 cups spinach
- 1 cup mixed berries
- 1/2 cup goat cheese
- 1/4 cup sliced almonds

METHOD

- Mix dressing ingredients in a small bowl.
- Layer ingredients in mason jar starting with dressing, then spinach, berries, cheese, and almonds.
- Seal and refrigerate until ready to eat.
- Shake before serving.

AUTUMN HARVEST SALAD

DRESSING INGREDIENTS

- 2 tbsp olive oil
- 1 tbsp apple cider vinegar
- 1 tsp honey

SALAD INGREDIENTS

- 2 cups mixed greens
- 1 cup diced apple
- 1/2 cup dried cranberries
- 1/2 cup walnuts

METHOD

- Mix dressing ingredients in a small bowl.
- Layer ingredients in mason jar starting with dressing, then greens, apple, cranberries, and walnuts.
- Seal and refrigerate until ready to eat.
- Shake before serving.

WINTER CITRUS SALAD

DRESSING INGREDIENTS

- 3 tbsp olive oil
- 1 tbsp orange juice
- Salt and pepper to taste

SALAD INGREDIENTS

- 2 cups mixed greens
- 1 cup sliced oranges
- 1/2 cup sliced fennel
- 1/4 cup sliced almonds

METHOD

- Mix dressing ingredients in a small bowl.
- Layer ingredients in mason jar starting with dressing, then greens, oranges, fennel, and almonds.
- Seal and refrigerate until ready to eat.
- Shake before serving.

SPRING ASPARAGUS SALAD

DRESSING INGREDIENTS

- 2 tbsp olive oil
- 1 tbsp lemon juice
- Salt and pepper to taste

SALAD INGREDIENTS

- 2 cups mixed greens
- 1 cup blanched asparagus
- 1/2 cup peas
- 1/2 cup feta cheese

METHOD

- Mix dressing ingredients in a small bowl.
- Layer ingredients in mason jar starting with dressing, then greens, asparagus, peas, and feta.
- Seal and refrigerate until ready to eat.
- Shake before serving.

SUMMER CORN SALAD

DRESSING INGREDIENTS

- 2 tbsp olive oil
- 1 tbsp lime juice
- Salt and pepper to taste

SALAD INGREDIENTS

- 2 cups mixed greens
- 1 cup corn
- 1 cup diced bell pepper
- 1/2 cup diced red onion

METHOD

- Mix dressing ingredients in a small bowl.
- Layer ingredients in mason jar starting with dressing, then greens, corn, bell pepper, and onion.
- Seal and refrigerate until ready to eat.
- Shake before serving.

AUTUMN PEAR SALAD

DRESSING INGREDIENTS

- 2 tbsp olive oil
- 1 tbsp apple cider vinegar
- 1 tsp honey

SALAD INGREDIENTS

- 1. 2 cups mixed greens
- 1 cup diced pear
- 1/2 cup blue cheese
- 1/4 cup walnuts

METHOD

- Mix dressing ingredients in a small bowl.
- Layer ingredients in mason jar starting with dressing, then greens, pear, cheese, and walnuts.
- Seal and refrigerate until ready to eat.
- Shake before serving.

WINTER ROOT VEGETABLE SALAD

DRESSING INGREDIENTS

- 3 tbsp olive oil
- 1 tbsp balsamic vinegar
- Salt and pepper to taste

SALAD INGREDIENTS

- 2 cups mixed greens
- 1 cup roasted root vegetables
- 1/2 cup goat cheese
- 1/4 cup pecans

METHOD

- Mix dressing ingredients in a small bowl.
- Layer ingredients in mason jar starting with dressing, then greens, root vegetables, cheese, and pecans.
- Seal and refrigerate until ready to eat.
- Shake before serving.

SPRING PEA AND RADISH SALAD

DRESSING INGREDIENTS

- 2 tbsp olive oil
- 1 tbsp lemon juice
- Salt and pepper to taste

SALAD INGREDIENTS

- 2 cups mixed greens
- 1 cup peas
- 1 cup sliced radishes
- 1/2 cup feta cheese

METHOD

- Mix dressing ingredients in a small bowl.
- Layer ingredients in mason jar starting with dressing, then greens, peas, radishes, and feta.
- Seal and refrigerate until ready to eat.
- Shake before serving.

SUMMER TOMATO AND CUCUMBER SALAD

DRESSING INGREDIENTS

- 3 tbsp olive oil
- 1 tbsp red wine vinegar
- Salt and pepper to taste

SALAD INGREDIENTS

- 2 cups mixed greens
- 1 cup cherry tomatoes
- 1 cup diced cucumber
- 1/2 cup feta cheese

METHOD

- Mix dressing ingredients in a small bowl.
- Layer ingredients in mason jar starting with dressing, then greens, tomatoes, cucumber, and feta.
- Seal and refrigerate until ready to eat.
- Shake before serving.

Around the World Mason Jar Salads

this section, we'll explore the flavors and ingredients of various cuisines, incorporating them into our mason jar salads. From the zesty and vibrant flavors of Mexico to the comforting and hearty ingredients of the Mediterranean, we'll create salads that not only nourish your body but also broaden your culinary horizons. So, get ready to pack your mason jars with a world of flavor. Let's embark on this delicious journey together!

ITALIAN PASTA SALAD

DRESSING INGREDIENTS

- Olive oil 3 tbsp
- Red wine vinegar 1 tbsp
- Dried oregano 1 tsp
- Salt and pepper to taste

SALAD INGREDIENTS

- Cooked pasta 1 cup
- Cherry tomatoes 1 cup
- Mozzarella balls 1/2 cup
- Sliced olives 1/2 cup
- Diced red onion 1/2 cup

METHOD

- Mix all dressing ingredients in a small bowl.
- Layer ingredients in mason jar starting with dressing. Follow with pasta, tomatoes, mozzarella, olives, and onion.
- Seal and refrigerate until ready to eat.
- Shake before serving.

MEXICAN BEAN SALAD

DRESSING INGREDIENTS

- Olive oil 2 tbsp
- Lime juice 1 tbsp
- Cumin 1 tsp
- Salt and pepper to taste

SALAD INGREDIENTS

- Cooked quino
- 1 cup, Black beans 1 cup
- Corn 1 cup
- Diced bell pepper 1
- Diced red onion 1/2 cup

METHOD

- Mix all dressing ingredients in a small bowl.
- Layer ingredients in mason jar starting with dressing. Follow with quinoa, beans, corn, bell pepper, and onion.
- Seal and refrigerate until ready to eat.
- Shake before serving.

DELUX GREEK SALAD

DRESSING INGREDIENTS

- Olive oil 3 tbsp, Red wine vinegar 1 tbsp, Dried oregano 1 tsp, Salt and pepper to taste

SALAD INGREDIENTS

- Diced cucumber 1 cup
- Cherry tomatoes 1 cup
- Sliced olives 1/2 cup
- Feta cheese 1/2 cup
- Diced red onion 1/2 cup
- Shredded chicken 1/2 cup

METHOD

- Mix all dressing ingredients in a small bowl.
- Layer ingredients in mason jar starting with dressing. Follow with cucumber, tomatoes, olives, feta, chicken and onion.
- Seal and refrigerate until ready to eat.
- Shake before serving.

JAPANESE SOBA NOODLE SALAD

DRESSING INGREDIENTS

- Sesame oil 2 tbsp
- Soy sauce 1 tbsp
- Rice vinegar 1 tbsp
- Honey 1 tsp
- Grated ginger 1 tsp

SALAD INGREDIENTS

- Cooked soba noodles 1 cup
- Shredded carrots 1 cup
- Sliced bell peppers 1 cup
- Edamame 1/2 cup
- Sliced green onions 1/2 cup

METHOD

- Mix all dressing ingredients in a small bowl.
- Layer ingredients in mason jar starting with dressing. Follow with noodles, carrots, bell peppers, edamame, and green onions.
- Seal and refrigerate until ready to eat.
- Shake before serving.

FRENCH NICOISE SALAD

DRESSING INGREDIENTS

- Olive oil 3 tbsp
- Lemon juice 1 tbsp
- Dijon mustard 1 tsp
- Salt and pepper to taste

SALAD INGREDIENTS

- Cooked green beans 1 cup
- Cherry tomatoes 1 cup,
- Sliced olives 1/2 cup
- Diced red onion 1/2 cup
- Boiled eggs 2

METHOD

- Mix all dressing ingredients in a small bowl.
- Layer ingredients in mason jar starting with dressing. Follow with green beans, tomatoes, olives, onion, and eggs.
- Seal and refrigerate until ready to eat.
- Shake before serving.

THAI QUINOA SALAD

DRESSING INGREDIENTS

- Olive oil 2 tbsp
- Lime juice 1 tbsp
- Soy sauce 1 tbsp
- Honey 1 tsp
- Grated ginger 1 tsp

SALAD INGREDIENTS

- Cooked quinoa 1 cup
- Shredded carrots 1 cup
- Sliced bell peppers 1 cup
- Edamame 1/2 cup
- Sliced green onions 1/2 cup

METHOD

- Mix all dressing ingredients in a small bowl.
- Layer ingredients in mason jar starting with dressing. Follow with quinoa, carrots, bell peppers, edamame, and green onions.
- Seal and refrigerate until ready to eat.
- Shake before serving.

INDIAN CHICKPEA SALAD

DRESSING INGREDIENTS

- Olive oil 2 tbsp
- Lemon juice 1 tbsp
- Curry powder 1 tsp
- Salt and pepper to taste

SALAD INGREDIENTS

- Cooked chickpeas 1 cup
- Diced cucumber 1 cup
- Diced red onion 1/2 cup
- Diced tomatoes 1/2 cup
- Fresh cilantro 1/4 cup

METHOD

- Mix all dressing ingredients in a small bowl.
- Layer ingredients in mason jar starting with dressing. Follow with chickpeas, cucumber, onion, tomatoes, and cilantro.
- Seal and refrigerate until ready to eat.
- Shake before serving.

MOROCCAN COUSCOUS SALAD

DRESSING INGREDIENTS

- Olive oil 2 tbsp
- Lemon juice 1 tbsp
- Cumin 1 tsp
- Salt and pepper to taste

SALAD INGREDIENTS

- Cooked couscous 1 cup
- Diced cucumber 1 cup
- Diced red onion 1/2 cup
- Diced tomatoes 1/2 cup
- Fresh mint 1/4 cup

METHOD

- Mix all dressing ingredients in a small bowl.
- Layer ingredients in mason jar starting with dressing. Follow with couscous, cucumber, onion, tomatoes, and mint.
- Seal and refrigerate until ready to eat.
- Shake before serving.

SPANISH GAZPACHO SALAD

DRESSING INGREDIENTS

- Olive oil 2 tbsp
- Red wine vinegar 1 tbsp
- Salt and pepper to taste

SALAD INGREDIENTS

- Diced cucumber 1 cup
- Diced red onion 1/2 cup
- Diced tomatoes 1 cup
- Diced bell pepper 1
- Fresh parsley 1/4 cup

METHOD

- Mix all dressing ingredients in a small bowl.
- Layer ingredients in mason jar starting with dressing. Follow with cucumber, onion, tomatoes, bell pepper, and parsley.
- Seal and refrigerate until ready to eat.
- Shake before serving.

VIETNAMESE VERMICELLI SALAD

DRESSING INGREDIENTS

- Lime juice 2 tbsp
- Fish sauce 1 tbsp
- Sugar 1 tsp
- Grated garlic 1 clove
- Grated ginger 1 tsp

SALAD INGREDIENTS

- Cooked vermicelli noodles 1 cup
- Shredded carrots 1 cup
- Sliced cucumber 1 cup
- Fresh mint 1/4 cup
- Fresh cilantro 1/4 cup

METHOD

- Mix all dressing ingredients in a small bowl.
- Layer ingredients in mason jar starting with dressing. Follow with noodles, carrots, cucumber, mint, and cilantro.
- Seal and refrigerate until ready to eat.
- Shake before serving.

In Conclusion

As we come to the end of this book, we hope you've found inspiration in these pages. We've journeyed through the world of mason jar salads together, exploring a variety of flavors, ingredients, and techniques. We've seen how simple ingredients can come together to create meals that are not only delicious but also nourishing and convenient.

We've learned that eating healthy doesn't have to be complicated or time-consuming. With a little bit of planning and a lot of creativity, we can create meals that satisfy our hunger, fuel our bodies, and delight our taste buds.

We've also seen how versatile mason jar salads can be. From vegetarian to protein-packed, from grain-based to fruit and nut, there's a mason jar salad for every taste, every dietary need, and every mood.

But more than that, we've seen how these salads can fit into our lives. They're perfect for busy weekdays, for lunches on the go, for meals enjoyed in the park or at the office. They're proof that fast food can be good food, and that eating well doesn't have to be a chore.

1.

As you continue your culinary journey, we encourage you to keep experimenting, to keep exploring. Try new ingredients, new flavor combinations. Use these recipes as a starting point, but don't be afraid to make them your own.

Remember, the goal is not perfection, but progress. It's about making choices that make you feel good, that nourish your body and your soul. It's about finding joy in the food you eat and the way you live.

So, keep your mason jars at the ready. Fill them with colorful veggies, hearty grains, lean proteins, and delicious dressings. Create meals that you look forward to, that satisfy your hunger, and that make you feel good.

Thank you for joining us on this culinary adventure. We hope this book has inspired you, empowered you, and most importantly, helped you discover the joy of healthy eating.

As you move forward, remember to enjoy the process. The chopping of the vegetables, the whisking of the dressing, the layering of the ingredients - these are all acts of self-care, small moments of mindfulness in our busy lives.

So, here's to health, to convenience, to delicious meals enjoyed anywhere and everywhere. Here's to mason jar salads, the humble heroes of the culinary world. Happy cooking, dear reader, and enjoy every bite!

Printed in Great Britain
by Amazon